First World War
and Army of Occupation
War Diary
France, Belgium and Germany

18 DIVISION
Divisional Troops
Divisional Cyclist Company
1 January 1915 - 21 May 1916

WO95/2024/2

The Naval & Military Press Ltd
www.nmarchive.com
Published in association with The National Archives

Published by

The Naval & Military Press Ltd

Unit 10 Ridgewood Industrial Park,

Uckfield, East Sussex,

TN22 5QE England

Tel: +44 (0) 1825 749494

www.naval-military-press.com

www.nmarchive.com

This diary has been reprinted in facsimile from the original. Any imperfections are inevitably reproduced and the quality may fall short of modern type and cartographic standards.

© **Crown Copyright**
Images reproduced by permission of The National Archives, London, England, 2015.

Contents

Document type	Place/Title	Date From	Date To
Heading	WO95/2024-2		
Heading	18th Division 18th Cyclist Coy. Jly 1915-May 1916		
Heading	18th Division 18th Div. Cycl. Coy. Vol I From July To November 1915		
Heading	War Diary of 18th Div Cyclist Company From 25/7/15 To 30/11/15 (Volume I)		
War Diary	Codford	25/07/1915	25/07/1915
War Diary	S'Hampton	25/07/1915	25/07/1915
War Diary	Havre	26/07/1915	26/07/1915
War Diary	Amiens	27/07/1915	27/07/1915
War Diary	Fleselles	27/07/1915	27/07/1915
War Diary	Codford	25/07/1915	25/07/1915
War Diary	S'Hampton	25/07/1915	25/07/1915
War Diary	Havre	26/07/1915	26/07/1915
War Diary	Amiens	27/07/1915	27/07/1915
War Diary	Fleselles	27/07/1915	27/07/1915
War Diary	Fleselles	01/08/1915	08/08/1915
War Diary	St Gratien	08/08/1915	21/08/1915
War Diary	Morlancourt	21/08/1915	22/08/1915
War Diary	Ville Sur Ancre	22/08/1915	22/08/1915
War Diary	Fleselles	01/08/1915	08/08/1915
War Diary	St Gratien	08/08/1915	21/08/1915
War Diary	Morlancourt	21/08/1915	22/08/1915
War Diary	Ville Sur Ancre	22/08/1915	18/09/1915
War Diary	Ribemont	18/09/1915	24/09/1915
War Diary	Ville Sur Ancre	01/09/1915	18/09/1915
War Diary	Ribemont	18/09/1915	30/11/1915
War Diary	Ribemont	01/11/1915	30/11/1915
Heading	18th Cyclist Vols 2		
War Diary	Ribemont	01/12/1915	31/12/1915
War Diary	Ribemont	01/01/1915	31/01/1915
Miscellaneous	XVIII Div Cyclist Jan 16 III		
Miscellaneous	Committee of Imperial Defence, 2, Whitehall Gardens, S.W. With the Secretary's Compliments. For the favour of distribution 18/5/18		
War Diary	Ribemont	01/01/1916	31/01/1916
War Diary	Ribemont	01/02/1916	01/02/1916
War Diary	Dernancourt	02/02/1916	29/02/1916
War Diary	Ribemont	01/02/1916	01/02/1916
War Diary	Dernancourt	02/02/1916	29/02/1916
War Diary	Corbie	01/03/1916	15/03/1916
War Diary	Etinehem	16/03/1916	31/03/1916
War Diary	Corbie	01/03/1916	15/03/1916
War Diary	Etinehem	16/03/1916	31/03/1916
War Diary	Corbie	01/03/1916	15/03/1916
War Diary	Etinehem	16/03/1916	31/03/1916
War Diary	Etinehem (Somme)	01/04/1916	29/04/1916
Heading	War Diary of 18th Divisional Cyclist Coy. From 1st May 1916 To 22nd May 1916 Volume Vol 7		
War Diary		01/05/1916	21/05/1916

WB 95/2024 (2)

4 (2)

18TH DIVISION

18TH CYCLIST COY.
JLY 1915-MAY 1916.

18th Division

18th Devon Regt.
Vol I

121/7635

From July to November 1915

May 16

Army Form C. 2118

WAR DIARY
or
INTELLIGENCE SUMMARY
(Erase heading not required.)

Instructions regarding War Diaries and Intelligence Summaries are contained in F. S. Regs., Part II. and the Staff Manual respectively. Title Pages will be prepared in manuscript.

Place	Date	Hour	Summary of Events and Information	Remarks and references to Appendices

Confidential

War Diary

of.

18th Div¹ Cyclist Company

From 25/7/15
To 30/11/15.

(Volume 1.)

July 1915

WAR DIARY
or
INTELLIGENCE SUMMARY

Army Form C. 2118

Place	Date	Hour	Summary of Events and Information	Remarks and references to Appendices
CODFORD	25	7AM	Entrained for SOUTHAMPTON.	RAR
S'HAMPTON		5PM	Embarked on H.M.H.T "LA MARGUERITE"	RAR
HAVRE	26	8AM	Disembarked — moved to No 5 Camp	RAR
-		10PM	Entrained	RAR
AMIENS	27	7AM	Detrained and moved by route march to	RAR
FLESELLES		4PM	Billeted in rest billets till end of month	RAR

Army Form C. 2118

WAR DIARY
or
INTELLIGENCE SUMMARY
(Erase heading not required.)

July 1915

18th Divne Cyclist Coy.

Instructions regarding War Diaries and Intelligence Summaries are contained in F.S. Regs., Part II. and the Staff Manual respectively. Title Pages will be prepared in manuscript.

Place	Date	Hour	Summary of Events and Information	Remarks and references to Appendices
CODFORD	25	7AM	Entrained for SOUTHAMPTON.	RAF
S'HAMPTON		5PM	Embarked on H.M.H.T "LA MARGUERITE"	RAF
HAVRE	26	8AM	Disembarked - moved to no 5 Camp	RAF
		10PM	Entrained	RAF
AMIENS	27	7AM	Detrained and moved by route march to	RAF
FLESELLES		4PM	Billeted in rest billets till end of month	RAF

WAR DIARY
or
INTELLIGENCE SUMMARY

(Erase heading not required.)

Army Form C. 2118

August 1915

Place	Date	Hour	Summary of Events and Information	Remarks and references to Appendices
FLESELLES	1st		In rest billets.	RAR
—	8th	3PM	Left billets	RAR
ST GRATIEN	8th	7PM	Moved into billets and remained here till 21/8.	RAR
—	21st	3PM	Left billets	RAR
MORLANCOURT	21st	5PM	Moved into billets	RAR
—	22nd	3...	Left billets	RAR
VILLE SUR ANCRE	22nd	7...	Moved into billets and remained to end of month	RAR

Army Form C. 2118

WAR DIARY
or
INTELLIGENCE SUMMARY
(Erase heading not required.)

18th Divl Cyclist Coy

August 1915

Place	Date	Hour	Summary of Events and Information	Remarks and references to Appendices
FLESELLES	1st		In rest billets.	RAR
-"-	8th	3 pm	Left billets	RAR
ST GRATIEN	8th	7 pm	Moved into billets and remained here till 21st	RAR
-"-	21st	3 pm	Left billets	RAR
MORLANCOURT	21st	5 pm	Moved into billets	RAR
	22nd	3 -"-	Left billets	RAR
VILLE SUR ANCRE	22nd	7 -"-	Moved into billets and remained to end of month.	RAR

WAR DIARY
or
INTELLIGENCE SUMMARY
(Erase heading not required.)

September 1915

Army Form C. 2118

Place	Date	Hour	Summary of Events and Information	Remarks and references to Appendices
VILLE SUR ANCRE	1st		In rest billets.	RAR
—	3rd		Nos 2 and 3 Platoons (Lt R.A Rochfort 2d L.A.H.HAWKINS and 2Lt G WAIGHT) attached to 53rd Bde for 7 days instruction in trenches	RAR
—	10th		Nos 1 and 6 Platoons (2Lt G.L.BLIGHT and Lt F.C.BOOTY) relieve Nos 2 + 3 Plat. & are in trenches for 7 days instruction	RAR
—	11th		Capt WAS ROUGH transferred to R.F.C. Command taken over by Lt R.A.ROCHFORT.	RAR
—	12th		2179 Cpl T.MORRIS wounded (right shoulder) and evacuated.	RAR
—	17th		Nos 4 and 5 Platoons (2Lt E.C.THOMPSON and 2Lt W F MORRIS) relieve Nos 1 and 6 platoons for 7 days instruction in trenches.	RAR
—	18th	2PM	Coy move to	RAR
RIBEMONT	18th.	3PM	Coy move into billets. 2Lt R.FRANKAU joins via ROUGH (honorary)	RAR
	24th		Nos 4 and 5 Platoons rejoin from trenches — Whole Coy in billets to end of month.	RAR

September 1915

WAR DIARY or INTELLIGENCE SUMMARY

Army Form C. 2118

18th Divne Cyclist Coy

Place	Date	Hour	Summary of Events and Information	Remarks and references to Appendices
VILLE SUR ANCRE	1st		In rest billets.	RAF
—	3rd		Nos 2 and 3 Platoons (2/Lt R.A Rochfort, 2/Lt A.H. HAWKINS and 2/Lt G. WAIGHT) attached to 53rd Bde for 7 days instruction in trenches	RAF
—	10th		Nos 1 and 6 Platoons (2/Lt G.L. BLIGHT and 2/Lt F.C. BOOTY) relieve Nos 2 & 3 Plat. 2ons in trenches for 7 days instruction	RAF
—	11th		Capt: WAS ROUGH transferred to R.F.C. Command taken over by 2/Lt R.A. ROCHFORT.	RAF
—	12th		2179 Cpl T. MORRIS wounded (right shoulder) and evacuated.	RAF
—	17th		Nos 4 and 5 Platoons (2/Lt G.C. THOMPSON and 2/Lt W.F. MORRIS) relieve Nos 1 and 6 platoons for 7 days instruction in trenches.	RAF
—	18th	2PM	Coy move to	RAF
RIBEMONT	18th	3PM	Coy move into billets. 2/Lt R. FRANKAU joins vice R.O.U.G.H (wound). Whole Coy in billets	RAF
—	24th		Nos 4 and 5 month Platoons rejoin from trenches.	RAF

Army Form C. 2118

October 1915

WAR DIARY
or
INTELLIGENCE SUMMARY
(Erase heading not required.)

Place	Date	Hour	Summary of Events and Information	Remarks and references to Appendices
RIBEMONT	1st		Coy in rest billets from 1st to 31st.	R.A.F

Army Form C. 2118

October 1915

18th Divre Cyc'l of Coy

WAR DIARY
or
INTELLIGENCE SUMMARY
(Erase heading not required.)

Instructions regarding War Diaries and Intelligence Summaries are contained in F. S. Regs., Part II. and the Staff Manual respectively. Title Pages will be prepared in manuscript.

Place	Date	Hour	Summary of Events and Information	Remarks and references to Appendices
RIDGEMONT	1st		Coy in rest billets from 1st to 31st	RAF

Army Form C. 2118

WAR DIARY
or
INTELLIGENCE SUMMARY
(Erase heading not required.)

November 1915

Place	Date	Hour	Summary of Events and Information	Remarks and references to Appendices
RIBEMONT	23rd		Coy in rest billets.	RAF
-,-	24th	8AM	Coy on trench digging - intermediate line - BECORDEL to 1p.m.	RAF
-,-	24th	8AM	Coy on trench digging - intermediate line - BECORDEL to 1p.m.	RAF
-,-	25th	8AM	Coy on trench digging - intermediate line - BECORDEL to 1.30PM	RAF
-,-	26th	8AM	Coy on trench digging - intermediate line - BECORDEL to 1.30PM	RAF
-,-		10AM	Air raid by three German aeroplanes - no casualties in the Coy.	RAF
-,-	27	8AM	Coy on trench digging - intermediate line - BECORDEL to 1.30PM	RAF
-,-	30	8AM	Coy on trench digging - intermediate line - BECORDEL to 1.30PM	RAF
-,-		8AM	No 3 platoon (2nd G WAIGHT) to ST GRATIEN for 14 days wood cutting	RAF

November 1915

Army Form C. 2118

18th Divn Cyclist Coy

WAR DIARY
or
INTELLIGENCE SUMMARY
(Erase heading not required.)

Place	Date	Hour	Summary of Events and Information	Remarks and references to Appendices
RIBEMONT	19th		Coy in rest billets.	RAR
—	23rd	8 AM	Coy on trench digging – intermediate line – BECORDEL to 1 p.m.	RAR
—	24th	8 AM	Coy on trench digging – intermediate line – BECORDEL to 1 p.m.	RAR
—	25th	8 AM	Coy on trench digging – intermediate line – BECORDEL to 1.30 PM	RAR
—	26	8 AM	Coy on trench digging – intermediate line – BECORDEL to 1.30 PM	RAR
—		10 AM	Attacked by three German aeroplanes – no casualties in the Coy.	RAR
—	27	8 AM	Coy on trench digging – intermediate line BECORDEL to 1.30 PM	RAR
—	30	8 AM	Coy on trench digging – intermediate line BECORDEL to 1.30 PM	RAR
—			No 3 platoon (Pte G WAIGHT) to SIGRATIEN for 14 days wood cutting	RAR

18th Exhib.
Vols. 2.

Army Form C. 2118

18TH DIVISIONAL CYCLIST COY.   WAR DIARY or
No% 19/15 INTELLIGENCE SUMMARY

(Erase heading not required.)

Instructions regarding War Diaries and Intelligence
Summaries are contained in F. S. Regs., Part II.
and the Staff Manual respectively. Title Pages
will be prepared in manuscript.

Place	Date	Hour	Summary of Events and Information	Remarks and references to Appendices
RIBEMONT	1st to 31st Oct 1918		Company in rest billets — employed on road making fatigue between BUIRE and MEAULTE from 8 AM to 3 PM daily. No 3 Platoon at ST GRATIEN woodcutting.	ADLS / RAF

Army Form C. 2118

WAR DIARY
or
INTELLIGENCE SUMMARY

18TH DIVISIONAL CYCLIST COY. Nov 1915

Place	Date	Hour	Summary of Events and Information	Remarks and references to Appendices
RIBEMONT	1st to 31st Nov		Company in rest billets – employed on road making fatigues between RIBEMONT & ST GRATIEN – Approx strength 3 PM daily	RAP / RAP

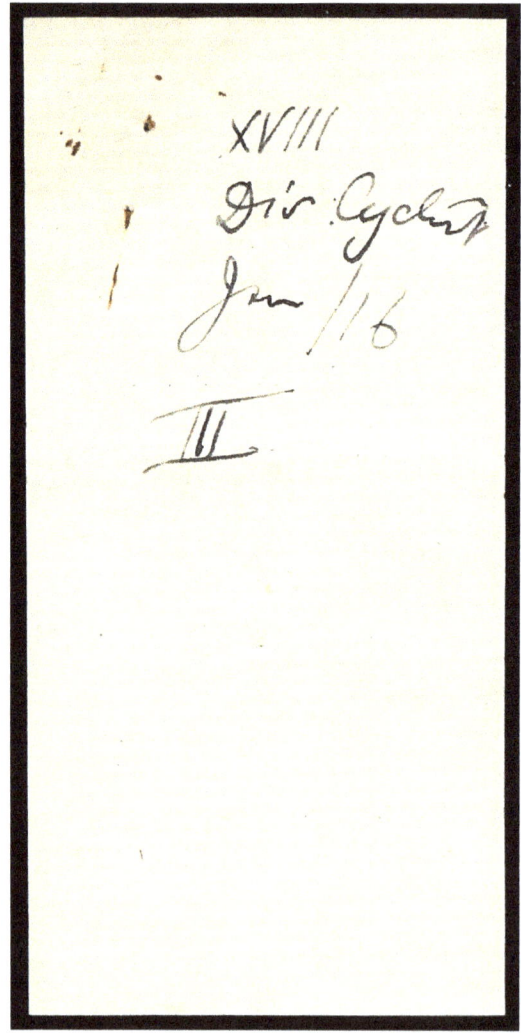

XVIII
Div. Cyclop
Jan /16

III

COMMITTEE OF IMPERIAL DEFENCE,
2, WHITEHALL GARDENS,
S.W.

With the Secretary's Compliments.

For the favour of

distribution.

18/5/16.

Army Form C. 2118

WAR DIARY
or
INTELLIGENCE SUMMARY
(Erase heading not required.)

18TH DIVISIONAL CYCLIST COY.

January 1916

Instructions regarding War Diaries and Intelligence Summaries are contained in F.S. Regs., Part II. and the Staff Manual respectively. Title Pages will be prepared in manuscript.

Place	Date 1916	Hour	Summary of Events and Information	Remarks and references to Appendices
RIBEMONT	1st to 31st Jan		Company in redoubts — employed roadmaking between BUIRE & HERNANCOURT. No 3 Platoon at ST GRATIEN woodcutting.	RAS RAS

RAFRochfort Capt

Army Form C. 2118

18TH DIVISIONAL CYCLIST COY. January 1916

WAR DIARY
or
INTELLIGENCE SUMMARY
(Erase heading not required.)

Instructions regarding War Diaries and Intelligence Summaries are contained in F.S. Regs., Part II. and the Staff Manual respectively. Title Pages will be prepared in manuscript.

Place	Date 1916	Hour	Summary of Events and Information	Remarks and references to Appendices
RIBEMONT	1st to 31st Jan		Company in real billets – employed roadmaking between BUIRE & DERNANCOURT. No 3 Platoon at ST GRATIEN woodcutting.	RAR RAR

R.A. Rochfort Capt.

R.A. Rochfort

Army Form C. 2118

WAR DIARY
or
INTELLIGENCE SUMMARY

(Erase heading not required.)

February 1916

Instructions regarding War Diaries and Intelligence Summaries are contained in F.S. Regs., Part II. and the Staff Manual respectively. Title Pages will be prepared in manuscript.

Place	Date	Hour	Summary of Events and Information	Remarks and references to Appendices
RIBEMONT	1st		Moved to DERNANCOURT.	R.A.R. O.A.R.
DERNAN COURT	2nd to 29th		Coy in wet weather employed on road fatigue	

Army Form C. 2118

WAR DIARY
or
INTELLIGENCE SUMMARY

(Erase heading not required.)

February  19/16

Instructions regarding War Diaries and Intelligence Summaries are contained in F. S. Regs., Part II. and the Staff Manual respectively. Title Pages will be prepared in manuscript.

Place	Date	Hour	Summary of Events and Information	Remarks and references to Appendices
RIBEMONT	14		Marched to DERNANCOURT	RJR
DERNAN COURT	2nd to 29th		Our men and mules employed on roads, fatigues	QM

Army Form C. 2118

WAR DIARY
or
INTELLIGENCE SUMMARY
(Erase heading not required.)

18's Divl Cyclist Coy.

March 1916.

Place	Date	Hour	Summary of Events and Information	Remarks and references to Appendices
CORBIE	1st		Company moved to rest billets.	RAR
"	2nd to 15/3/16		Employed on Quarry & road metal at CORBIE Quarry	RAR
ETINEHEM	16th 3/		moved to ETINEHEM. Employed on fatigue under C.R.E. 18's Divn.	RAR

RMRochfort Capt

18TH DIVISION

18th Divn Cyclist Coy

March 1916

Army Form C. 2118

WAR DIARY
or
INTELLIGENCE SUMMARY

(Erase heading not required.)

Place	Date	Hour	Summary of Events and Information	Remarks and references to Appendices
CORBIE	1st		Company moved to rest billets.	AAA
"	2nd to 15th		Employed on quarrying road metal at CORBIE quarry	AAA AAA
ETINEHEM	16th 31st		Moved to ETINEHEM. Employed on fatigues on roads. Under C.R.E., 18th Divn.	AAA

18th Army Cyclist Bn

Army Form C. 2118

WAR DIARY
or
INTELLIGENCE SUMMARY
(Erase heading not required.)

Instructions regarding War Diaries and Intelligence Summaries are contained in F. S. Regs., Part II. and the Staff Manual respectively. Title Pages will be prepared in manuscript.

Place	Date	Hour	Summary of Events and Information	Remarks and references to Appendices
CORBIE	1st June 7th 15th		Composing with 18th Corps Cyclists & Company. General training.	BM AB RAR
ETINEHEM	16th 31st		Moved to ETINEHEM. Employed on fatigues in various areas G.R.E., 18 Division.	

APRIL 1916

WAR DIARY
or
INTELLIGENCE SUMMARY

(Erase heading not required.)

Army Form C. 2118

18th Divn Cyclist Coy

Vol 6

Place	Date	Hour	Summary of Events and Information	Remarks and references to Appendices
ETINEHEM (SOMME)	1st		Company still employed on road-making fatigues under C.R.E. 18th Divn. One platoon a day carried out four hours training.	GRB.
	16th		A party was detailed each night to work on the road leading from the PERONNE road to CARNOY, being under observation in daylight from the German lines. Work was done from midnight until dawn.	GRB
	29		The night road party stopped. A platoon (Lt. G.L. Bright) proceeded to GUILLAUCOURT for fatigue in the trench area.	GRB.

Army Form C. 2118

APRIL 1916

WAR DIARY
or
INTELLIGENCE SUMMARY
(Erase heading not required.)

18th Divl Cyclist Coy.

Place	Date	Hour	Summary of Events and Information	Remarks and references to Appendices
ETINEHEM (SOMME)	1st		Company still employed on road-making fatigues under C.R.E. 18th Divn. a day carried out four hours training.	GHB.
	16th		One platoon was detailed each night to work on the road leading from the PERONNE road to CARNOY, being under observation in daylight from the German lines. Work was done from midnight until dawn.	GHB.
	29th		The night road party stopped. A platoon (Lt. G.L. (Blight-) proceeded to GUILLAUCOURT for fatigue in the French area.	GHB.

(18) 18 Div Cycles Vol 7

Confidential

War Diary

of

18th Divisional Cyclist Coy.

from 1st May 1916 to 22nd May, 1916.

Volume.

Army Form C. 2118.

18th Divisional Gelin Coy

WAR DIARY
or
INTELLIGENCE SUMMARY.
(Erase heading not required.)

Hour, Date, Place	Summary of Events and Information	Remarks and references to Appendices
May 1916 1st – 4th	Company engaged on road fatigue for CRE 18th Div and billeted at ETEINEHEM.	
4th – 14th	Coy engaged on fatigue for XIII Corps at MONTIERS	
14th	Coy billeted at ALLERY-SUR-SOMME. Capt RA ROCHFORT relinquishes command of Coy. Coy taken over by Lt GL BLIGHT for Lt WF MORRIS who is on leave of absence.	
14th – 21st	Coy Engaged on road fatigue for CRE 18th Div (a) Billeted at GROVETOWN CAMP, BRAY	
21st	Coy moved to VAUX-SUR-SOMME and became part of XII Corps Gelin Batt.	

www.ingramcontent.com/pod-product-compliance
Lightning Source LLC
Chambersburg PA
CBHW081502160426

43193CB00014B/2568